William Wells

The original United States warship

William Wells

The original United States warship

ISBN/EAN: 9783337174965

Printed in Europe, USA, Canada, Australia, Japan

Cover: Foto ©ninafisch / pixelio.de

More available books at **www.hansebooks.com**

THE STORY
OF THE
MONITOR

THE FIRST NAVAL CONFLICT BETWEEN IRON CLAD VESSELS.

ISSUED BY THE

CORNELIUS S. BUSHNELL
NATIONAL MEMORIAL ASSOCIATION
NEW HAVEN, CONN.

1899

THE ORIGINAL UNITED STATES WARSHIP

"MONITOR."

COPIES OF CORRESPONDENCE BETWEEN THE LATE

CORNELIUS S. BUSHNELL,

OF NEW HAVEN, CONN.,

CAPTAIN JOHN ERICSSON

AND

Hon. GIDEON WELLES, Secretary of the United States Navy,

TOGETHER WITH A BRIEF SKETCH OF MR. BUSHNELL'S LIFE.

————————

ERICSSON, BUSHNELL, GRISWOLD AND WINSLOW, CONTRACTORS WITH THE
GOVERNMENT.
THOS. F. ROWLAND, BUILDER OF HULL AND TURRET.
C. H. DELAMETER & CO., BUILDERS OF ENGINES, BOILERS AND MACHINERY.
DANIEL DREW AND NEHEMIAH D. SPERRY, OF NEW HAVEN, BONDSMEN.

RECORDS SHOWING HOW THE PLANS OF THE MONITOR WERE
URGED UPON THE GOVERNMENT AND FINALLY ADOPTED.

WITH PORTRAITS, ILLUSTRATIONS AND COPIES OF CONTRACTS
FOR VESSEL'S CONSTRUCTION

COMPILED BY

WILLIAM S. WELLS,

(LATE) 2ND ASSISTANT ENGINEER U. S. NAVY,
UNDER DIRECTIONS OF THE CORNELIUS S. BUSHNELL NATIONAL MEMORIAL
ASSOCIATION.

NEW HAVEN, CONN., SEPTEMBER, 1899.

THIS COMPILATION

IS RESPECTFULLY DEDICATED

TO

SERENO S. BUSHNELL,

REV. SAMUEL C. BUSHNELL,

MRS. CHARLOTTE BUSHNELL WATSON,

CORNELIUS J. BUSHNELL,

NATHAN BUSHNELL,

ERICSSON E. BUSHNELL,

WINTHROP G. BUSHNELL,

EDWARD W. BUSHNELL,

CHILDREN OF THE LATE CORNELIUS S. BUSHNELL.

PREFACE.

As long as the history of the United States shall endure, the thrilling story of the battle of March 9, 1862, between the "Monitor" and "Merrimac" will retain its fascination.

The people of this country and the nations of the world have not really known the full story and the real spirit or energy to which we are primarily indebted for urging the construction of this initial and then invincible vessel whose first encounter marked an epoch in the development of armaments afloat and ashore. And although thirty-seven years have passed since that memorable battle, and articles innumerable in books and magazines have appeared from time to time in regard to the building of this first type of modern war vessel, it has remained until this day to compile and present herewith some information heretofore unpublished in full, which will show that it was through the efforts of one man chiefly (the late Cornelius S. Bushnell of New Haven) that the work was accomplished.

The following pages will show that it was Mr. Bushnell's untiring energy and patriotic devotion which vigorously pushed the plans of Captain John Ericsson to final completion with not an hour to spare, and which operated in a large degree to lift the gloom that hung over the country during one of the darkest days of our history as a nation.

Mr. C. S. Bushnell was a citizen of New Haven, Conn., and his townsmen with many others desire to perform a duty due to his work and worth, by erecting a suitable memorial, to cost $25,000. The State of Connecticut has generously appropriated $5,000 towards the expense.

A committee of our foremost citizens, not only of this State, but throughout the country, has undertaken the task of erecting this monument, and now gives the country and the State an opportunity of showing their substantial appreciation of that in which we, as Americans, take such great pride, and which has been of such vast benefit to the United States, as well as to all civilized nations of the world.

Contributions may be sent to The New Haven Trust Co., Mr. T. Attwater Barnes, President; First National Bank Building, New Haven, Conn., Treasurer of the Cornelius S. Bushnell National Memorial Association.

CORNELIUS SCRANTON BUSHNELL.

1862.

THE BUILDING OF THE "MONITOR"

WITH

A SYNOPSIS OF THE LIFE OF CORNELIUS S. BUSHNELL.

In this country, it is not the accident of birth that gives a man sure and permanent distinction. His achievements, which have benefited humanity and marked steps in the world's progress, are the measure of the honor accorded him while living, and of the pride and reverence in which his memory is held when dead.

Upon this roll of citizens entitled to high honor for personal worth and public service, the name of CORNELIUS SCRANTON BUSHNELL should have especial prominence. He was born in Madison, Conn., July 19, 1829; died in New York city May 6, 1896, and was laid to rest May 9, in Evergreen Cemetery, New Haven, Conn.

His father, Nathan Bushnell, and his mother, Chloe Scranton, were respectively descended from Francis Bushnell and John Scranton, who emigrated from England to the New Haven Colony in 1638, and were members of the company which purchased the Guilford plantation from the Indians.

His youth was such as to develop an inherited strong body, and the influence of his home instilled into his mind the foundation of a sterling character.

He was an extraordinary man, a typical example of American pertinacity and versatile ability. Larger in stature and physical development than ordinary men, he excelled them also in activity and the power of comprehending great things.

His commercial foresight and appreciation of special merits in mechanical inventions were the marked characteristics of his eventful life, and enabled him to accomplish much for which the people of this country and the world should be profoundly grateful. At the age of 15 he began his life work on a coasting vessel and one year later was in command of a sixty-ton schooner. He remained in the coastwise trade five years, when he established his home in New Haven.

At the age of 21 he married Emily Fowler Clark, who died Jan. 10, 1869. The result of this marriage was the birth of nine sons and one daughter. Seven of the sons and one daughter survive him; also his widow by a later marriage.

He was for a time associated with his brother, N. T. Bushnell, in the grocery business. In 1858 the New Haven and New London railroad became embarrassed for want of revenue. Mr. Bushnell became interested, and perceived that the only way to put the road on a paying basis was to make a connection with lines to the eastward. Through his efforts and the great assistance of James I. Day, of Stonington, Giles F. Ward, of Saybrook, Conn., and other friends, legislative and financial support was obtained for building the road from New London to Stonington. He was made president.

The importance of this new through mail route between Boston and New York required his presence in Washington at this time, and brought him in close contact with the executive officials of the government.

The War of the Rebellion was seen to be inevitable. The city was filled with disloyal conspirators, and our national officials and property were practically without security or defence. When Fort Sumter was fired upon, he, with others, sojourning in the city, and some loyal residents, enlisted in the "Clay Battalion" for the purpose of guarding public buildings and the residences of officials until reinforcements could arrive.

His "muster into" the service bears date April 18, and his "muster out" is dated May 4, 1861. He, however, informed the writer that he performed service from April 13th. His discharge bears the signature of President Lincoln, and that of Simon Cameron, Secretary of War, with the expression of their thanks for services rendered at that critical time. (See fac-simile of discharge in Appendix.) This service made Mr. Bushnell eligible for membership in the Grand Army of the Republic, and he was duly mustered into Admiral Foote Post, No. 17, Dept. of Conn., G. A. R., on June 5, 1886, and was buried with Grand Army honors.

He was one of the organizers of the Union Pacific Railroad Company, and a potent factor in pushing this great enterprise to completion. He alone of the original organizers remained from start to finish in this important work.

He amassed a great fortune in this and other enterprises; but later, he was unfortunate in advancing capital for certain enterprises, especially the construction of the Atlantic and Southern Pacific Railroad, the development of iron works, mines and coal lands, etc., and in giving endorsements and guarantee bonds. Like many, he recognized too late the reaction of the stimulus given by the inflated finances of the war, and suffered the loss of nearly all he had accumulated.

Mr. Bushnell early saw that the Civil War was inevitable. He aprehended the magnitude it might assume, and foresaw the important part our forces afloat would have to take in the conflict. He seems to have been providentially selected to take a most important (although in the public eye an inconspicuous) part in this great struggle. He appreciated the value and necessity of sea power, offensive and defensive, and that it must be provided quickly.

With the expert assistance of S. H. Pook, a naval constructor of Boston, the plan of the ironclad "Galena" was developed, and with the coöperation of Hon. James E. English, member of Congress from New Haven, he received a contract to build this vessel. Mr. Bushnell also established a shipyard at Fair Haven, Conn., and built many steam and other vessels under the superintendency of Mr. Pook.

It was while consulting mechanical engineers as to the probable stability of the "Galena" that the most momentous incident in Mr. Bushnell's life occurred; his meeting with John Ericsson, of New York. Not only was this a most fortunate incident for the welfare of our Union of States, but it was productive of an epoch in the world's naval history. After Mr. Ericsson had shown him the plans of the Monitor, Mr. Bushnell at once comprehended the value of that novel vessel. He acted quickly, and his sterling patriotism and energy were proven by his instant approval and vigorous advocacy of this new and untried type of warship. With untiring wit and consummate tact he forced upon our government the adoption of the impregnable TURRET which has become standard with the navies of the world.

As one of the *sureties* to the United States Government for the *satisfactory* performance of the "MONITOR," with the Hon.

CAPT. JOHN ERICSSON.

N. D. Sperry, our present Congressman, and the late Daniel Drew, of New York, bondsmen, CORNELIUS SCRANTON BUSHNELL risked everything he possessed on the success or failure of a craft derided by one of the Naval Board at Washington as being "unlike anything in the heavens above, the earth beneath, or in the waters under the earth." The story of the memorable battle between the Monitor and the Merrimac in Hampton Roads, Va., on March 9, 1862, need not be repeated here.

The following copies of the original documents reveal clearly how the plans of Mr. Ericsson were unexpectedly brought to light, and how they were promptly carried to completion through the efforts of Mr. Bushnell, who, for a period of fifteen years after the conflict, was singularly modest and reticent in regard to the part he took in those stirring times. He used to say that history would take care of itself after he was gone. But in February, 1877, to make a record for history, and at the earnest solicitation of his friends, among them Hon. Gideon Welles, late Secretary of the Navy, he addressed a letter to Mr. Welles, reciting the story of his efforts which led up to the Monitor's construction. But before sending it to Mr. Welles and to make sure there were no statements contained in it that would not meet with the entire approval of Captain Ericsson, the letter was first sent to the inventor for his criticism.

Ericsson F. Bushnell, a son whom Mr. Bushnell had named after the inventor, was given permission to forward the letter to Captain Ericsson, as he desired to receive an autograph letter in reply.

Captain Ericsson returned the letter March 2, 1877, saying he did "not think that any changes or additions were needed, the main facts being well stated." (See fac simile copy of Captain Ericsson's letter in Appendix.)

The narrative was then sent to Gideon Welles, whose letter in reply, dated March 19, 1877 (printed in Appendix in facsimile for the first time) was in entire harmony with the letter written by Captain Ericsson and fully corroborated Mr. Bushnell's recital of the facts and accorded him full credit for his timely assistance to the Navy Department and to the nation.

The following is the letter to Hon. Gideon Welles, Secretary of the Navy:

HON. GIDEON WELLES :

Dear Sir:—Sometime since, during a short conversation in regard to the little *first Monitor*, you expressed a desire to learn from me some of the unwritten details of her history; particularly, how the plan of the boat came to be presented to the Government and the manner in which the contract for her construction was secured.

You doubtless remember handing me in August, 1861, at Willard's Hotel in Washington, D. C., the draft of a Bill which you desired Congress should pass, in reference to obtaining some kind of ironclad vessels to meet the formidable preparations the Rebels were making at Norfolk, Mobile and New Orleans. At that time you stated that you had already called the attention of Congress to this matter, but without effect.

I presented this Bill to the Hon. James E. English, Member of Congress from my District, who fortunately was on the Naval Committee, and untiringly urged the matter on their attention. The Chairman of the Committee, A. H. Rice, of Massachusetts, also coöperated most heartily, so that in about thirty days, if I remember correctly, the Bill passed both Houses and was immediately signed by President Lincoln. The Bill required all plans of ironclad vessels to be submitted to a Board of Naval Officers, appointed by yourself. The Board consisted of Admirals Smith and Paulding and Captain Davis, who examined hundreds of plans, good and bad, and among others that of a plated iron gunboat called the "*Galena*," contrived by Samuel H. Pook, now a constructor in the Navy Department. The partial protection of iron bars proposed for her seemed so burdensome that many naval officers warned me against the possibility of the "Galena's" being able to carry the additional weight of her armament.

C. H. Delamater, of New York, advised me to consult with the Engineer, Capt. John Ericsson, on the matter. This I proceeded at once to do, and on supplying him with the data necessary for his calculations promptly gained the answer, "She will easily carry the load you propose and stand a six inch shot—if fired from a respectable distance." At the close of this interview, Captain Ericsson asked if I had time just then to examine the plan of a floating battery absolutely impregnable to the heaviest shot or shell. I replied that this problem had been occupying me for the last three months, and that considering the time required for the construction, the Galena was the best result I had been able to obtain. He then placed before me the plan of the *Monitor;* explaining how quickly and powerfully she could be built, and exhibiting with characteristic pride a medal and letter of thanks received from Napoleon III. For it appears that Ericsson had invented the Battery when France and Russia were at war, and out of hostility to Russia had presented it to France, hoping thereby to aid the defeat of Sweden's hereditary foe. The invention, however came too late to be of service and was preserved for another issue.

You no doubt remember my delight with the plan of the Monitor when first Captain Ericsson entrusted it to my care; how I followed you to Hartford and astounded you by saying that the country was safe because I had found a Battery which would make us masters of the situation so far as the ocean was concerned. You were much pleased, and urged me to lose no time in presenting the plan to the Naval Board at Washington. I secured

"MERRIMAC" RAMMING U. S. FRIGATE "CUMBERLAND," MARCH 8, 1862.

"MONITOR" DEFENDING U. S. FRIGATE "CONGRESS," MARCH 9, 1862.

From Harper's Young People

Copyright, 1890, by Harper & Brothers

at once the coöperation of wise and able associates in the persons of the late Hon. John A. Griswold, of New York, and John F. Winslow, of Troy, both of them friends of Governor Seward and large manufacturers of iron plates, etc. Governor Seward furnished us with a strong letter of introduction to President Lincoln, who was at once greatly pleased with the simplicity of the plan and agreed to accompany us to the Navy Department at 11 A. M. the following day and aid us as best he could. He was on hand promptly at 11 o'clock the day before you returned from Hartford. Captain Fox, together with a part of the Naval Board, were present. All were surprised at the novelty of the plan. Some advised trying it, others ridiculed it. The conference was finally closed for that day by Mr. Lincoln's remarking, "All I have to say is what the girl said when she put her foot into the stocking, 'It strikes me there's something in it.'"

The following day Admiral Smith convened the full Board, when I presented, as best I could, the plan and its merits, carefully noting the remarks of each member of the Board. I then went to my hotel quite sanguine of success, but only to be disappointed on the following day. For during the hours following the last session, I found that the air had been thick with croakings that the Department was about to father another Ericsson failure. Never was I more active than now in the effort to prove that Ericsson had *never* made a failure. That, on the contrary, he had built for the Government the first steam war propeller ever made; that the bursting of the gun was no fault of his, but of the shell, which had not been made strong enough to prevent its flattening up with the pressure of the explosion behind it, making the bursting of the gun unavoidable; that his caloric principle was a triumphant success, but that no metal had yet been found to utilize it on a large scale. I succeeded at length in getting Admirals Smith and Paulding to promise to sign a report advising the building of one trial battery, *provided* Captain Davis would join with them. On going to him I was informed that "I might take the little thing home and worship it, as it would not be idolatry, because it was made in the image of nothing in the heaven above, or in the earth below, or in the waters under the earth." One thing only yet remained which it was possible to do. This was to get Ericsson to come to Washington and plead the case himself. This I was sure would *win* the case, and so informed you, for Ericsson is a full electric battery in himself. You at once promised to have a meeting in your room if I could succeed in inducing him to come. This was exceedingly doubtful, for so badly had he been treated and so unmercifully maligned in regard to the "*Princeton,*" that he had repeatedly declared that he would never set foot in Washington again.

Nevertheless, I appeared at his house the next morning precisely at 9 o'clock and heard his sharp greeting:

"Well? How is it?"

"Glorious," said I.

"Go on, go on!" said he, with impatience; "what did they say?"

"Admiral Smith says it is worthy of the genius of an Ericsson." The pride fairly gleamed in his eyes.

"But Paulding, what did he say of it?"

He said: "It's *just the* thing to clear the 'Rebs' out of Charleston with."

14

" How about Davis ?" he inquired, as I appeared to hesitate a moment.

" Oh, Davis," said I, " he wanted two or three explanations in detail which I could not give him, and so Secretary Welles proposed that I should come and get you to come to Washington and explain these few points to the entire Board in his room to-morrow."

" Well, I'll go—I'll go to-night."

From that moment I knew the success of the affair was assured. You remember how he thrilled every person present in your room with his vivid description of what the little boat would be and what she could do; that in ninety days' time she could be built, although the Rebels had already been four months at work on the Merrimac, with all the appliances of the Norfolk Navy Yard to help them.

You asked him how much it would cost to complete her. "Two hundred and seventy-five thousand dollars," he said. Then you promptly turned to the members of the Board, and one by one asked them if they would recommend that a contract be entered into for her construction with Captain Ericsson and his associates. Each one answered, ' Yes, by all means." Then you told Captain Ericsson to start her immediately. On the next day in New York a large portion of every article used in her construction was ordered, and a contract at once entered into between Captain Ericsson and his associates and T. F. Rowland at Greene Point for the expeditious construction of the most formidable vessel ever made. It was arranged that after a few days I should procure a formal documentary contract from the Naval Board, to be signed and executed by the Secretary of the Navy, Capt. John Ericsson and associates.

I regret that this part of the matter has been misunderstood, as though you had made terms heavier or the risk greater than you ought. The simple fact was that after we had entered upon the work of construction and before the formal contract had been awarded, a great clamor arose, much of it due to interested parties, to the effect that the Battery would prove a failure and disgrace the members of the Board for their action in recommending it. For their own protection, therefore, and out of their superabundant caution, they insisted on inserting in the contract a clause requiring us to guarantee the complete success of the Battery, so that in case she proved a failure the government might be refunded the amounts advanced to us from time to time during her construction. To Captain Ericsson and myself this was never an embarrassment. But to Mr. Winslow, as indeed to Mr. Griswold also, it appeared that the Board had asked too much. But I know that the noble old Admiral Smith never intended that we should suffer, and among the many fortunate things for which the nation had occasion to be grateful—such as the providential selection as President in those dark days of the immortal Lincoln and his wisely-chosen Cabinet—was the appointment of Admiral Smith to the charge of the navy yards, who always seemed to sleep with one eye open, so constant was his watchfulness and so eager his desire that the entire navy should always be in readiness to do its part in the overthrow of the Rebellion.

I am confident that no native-born child of this country will ever forget the proud son of Sweden, who could sit in his own house and contrive the

15

CREW OF THE "MONITOR" ON DECK AFTER HER BATTLE WITH THE MERRIMAC,

IMPRESSION OF A SHOT ON TURRET.

three thousand different parts that go to make up the complete hull of the steam battery "Dictator," so that when the mechanics came to put the parts together, not a single alteration in any particular was required to be made. What the little first Monitor and the subsequent larger ones achieved is a part of history.

One of my associates, as noble and generous a man as it is the lot of one ever to meet on earth, has gone to his rest—John A. Griswold—and fast shall we each and all follow, but it may be a pleasure to those that shall love our memory to find with your preserved records of those trying times this memorandum of the unrecorded private negotiations that resulted in the opportune meeting of the "cheesebox on the raft" with the ponderous Merrimac at Hampton Roads, March 9, 1862.

Very respectfully,

C. S. BUSHNELL.

NEW HAVEN, Conn., March 9, 1877.

Captain Ericsson's reply, certifying to the accuracy of the letter of Mr. C. S. Bushnell to Gideon Welles, printed above, was as follows :

NEW YORK, March 2, 1877.

My Dear Sir:—I have read with much pleasure your father's statement to Mr. Welles concerning the construction of the original Monitor. I do not think that any changes or additions are needed, the main facts being well stated.

Allow me to call your attention to the fact that your name should be spe't with a single *c*.

Please find your father's paper enclosed.

Yours very truly,

J. ERICSSON.

ERICSSON F. BUSHNELL, ESQ.,
New Haven.

A fac-simile of this letter appears in the Appendix.

Mr. Welles' reply to Mr. Bushnell's letter was as follows :

HARTFORD, 19th March, 1877.

C. S. BUSHNELL, ESQ.:

My Dear Sir:—I received on the 16th inst. your interesting communication, without date—relative to the construction of the Monitor. Many of the incidents narrated by you I remember, although more than fifteen years have gone by since they transpired. Some errors, not very essential and caused by lapse of years, occur,—Sedgwick, not Rice, was chairman of the Naval Committee; Griswold resided in Troy, not New York, and subsequently represented the Troy district in Congress, etc., etc.

I well remember asking you to put in writing the facts in your possession concerning the construction of the Monitor. Some statements of General Butler, Wendell Phillips and others to disparage the Navy Department, prevent the truth and deny us all credit, led Admiral Smith, in the Autumn of 1868. to address to me a communication, reciting the facts, for, he said, when we were gone, those of us who took the responsibility and would have incurred the disgrace had Ericsson's invention proved a failure, would be ignored and history misstated. As you were more intimate with the case at its inception—were the first to bring it to the attention of the Department, it seemed to me proper that your recollections and knowledge of the transaction should be reduced to writing. I am greatly obliged to you for the full and satisfactory manner in which you have complied with my request. Next, after Ericsson himself, you are entitled to the credit of bringing his invention to the knowledge of the Department. I would not, knowingly, do injustice to any one, and I am well aware that the official in civil life, and who in administering the government directs movements by which naval and military men acquire renown, is often by the passing multitude little thought of and scarcely known, but the truth should not be suppressed.

The civilians of the Navy Department, who adopted and pursued through ridicule and assault the Monitor experiment, Butler and others would slight and defame. In the history of the war, the Navy Department, which originated, planned and carried forward the naval achievements from Hatteras to New Orleans, and finally Fort Fisher, is scarcely known or mentioned. The heroes who fought the battles and periled their lives to carry into effect the plan which the Department devised have, deservedly, honorable remembrance, but the originators and movers are little known.

I remember, my dear sir, your earnest efforts in the early days of the war, and the comfort they gave me.

Yours,
GIDEON WELLES.

A fac-simile of this letter appears in the Appendix.

In August, 1885, Egbert Watson & Son, publishers of the "Mechanical Engineer" of New York, addressed to Mr. Bushnell a series of questions in regard to the construction of the Monitor and the following is a copy of the reply, dated Madison, Conn., August 19, 1885, together with the acknowledgment, dated August 20, 1885:

EGBERT WATSON & SON:

Gentlemen:—Your favor of August 15th came duly to hand. In reply I submit the following answers to your questions:

Question 1st. Is this the same Galena about which Mr. Winslow claims to have been in Washington, when you introduced the Monitor plans to him?
Answer. Yes.

Question 2d. Had it then been decided to build the Galena?
Answer. Yes.

Question 3d. Had Winslow or Griswold any interest in (your) obtaining the Galena contract?
Answer. Yes, for I promised to employ them to plate the vessel in case I succeeded in obtaining the contract for her construction.

THE MONITOR.

DESIGNED BY JOHN ERICSSON.   BUILT AT THE "CONTINENTAL
IRON WORKS," GREENPOINT, L. I., 1861.

SIDE ELEVATION.

DECK PLAN.

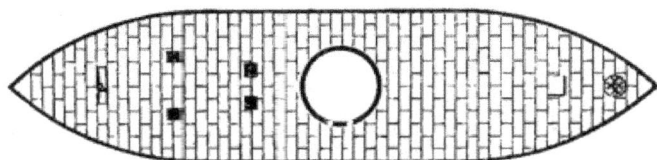

TRANSVERSE SECTION OF HULL AND TURRET.

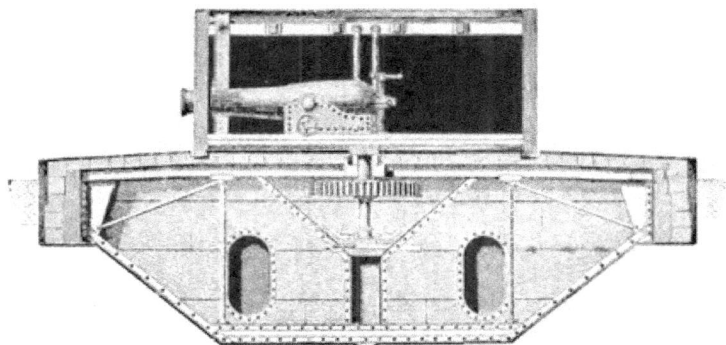

Question 4th.   Were they associated with you in it?

Answer.   Not otherwise than as just explained, viz., sub-contractors to plate her hull.

Question 5th.   Had you any relations with them that induced you to desire their aid in the Monitor matter apart from their acquaintance with the Secretaries of War, State and Navy?

Answer.   No.

Question 6th.   What date was Delamater present?

Answer.   I am not able at this time to give exact dates of any of these transactions, as I have no documents at hand with which to verify them. I met Mr. C. H. Delamater on the steps of Willard's hotel, Washington, just after I had secured the contract for the Galena. When I told him that several naval men doubted whether the vessel would be able to carry the stipulated amount of iron, he advised me to consult Capt. John Ericsson, of New York.

Question 7th.   Did you personally know Captain Ericsson at that time?

Answer.   No, nor had ever had any relations with him of any kind; but acting upon the advice of Mr. Delamater, I went to New York on the following day and laid the plans of the Galena before him, asking him whether the vessel would be able to carry the specified armor. He told me to call the next day for his answer. This I did and found everything satisfactory. Before I left he asked if I would like to examine the plans of a Battery absolutely impregnable to shot or shell. I told him that I had been working for several months to obtain the best naval defence possible, with the Galena—an iron-plated wooden vessel—as the result. He then produced a small dust-covered box containing the model and plans for the Monitor, which he fully explained in detail. I was satisfied at once that the naval defence, which our country so greatly needed, had been found, and perfectly overjoyed, when, at the close of the interview, Captain Ericsson entrusted the box with its precious contents to my care.

Question 8th.   How soon after the receipt of the plans of the Monitor was an interview had with Secretary Welles, and where?

Answer.   On the following day, at Hartford, Conn. I left New York that night, and went to Hartford direct, without stopping at my home in New Haven, so eager was I to save time in bringing this great discovery to the knowledge of the Navy Department. Secretary Welles, who was spending a few days at Hartford, was delighted with the invention, and asked me to take the plan immediately to Washington, and present it to the Naval Board.

Question 9th.   Before going to Washington, did you call on Captain Ericsson, and at what date?

Answer.   I think I did, but am not sure.

Question 10th.   On what date did you arrive in Washington?

Answer.   I cannot remember the exact date.

Question 11th.   Was the Monitor plan submitted to the Board before you interested Winslow and Griswold in it?

Answer.   No, it was not. Immediately on reaching Washington I laid the plans before Messrs. Winslow and Griswold, offering them a half interest in the enterprise, retaining a half interest for Captain Ericsson and myself, Ericsson having given me the liberty of making whatever terms I pleased. I selected these gentlemen because of their large acquaintance with Government authorities, and because I already had business relations with them, having contracted with them to plate the Galena.

Question 12th. When was Seward's letter obtained?

Answer. On the day after Winslow and Griswold agreed to unite with Ericsson and me in trying to secure a contract for the building of the Monitor.

Question 13th. What date was the first interview with President Lincoln?

Answer. I cannot give the date. It occurred the (same) day we secured Secretary Seward's letter of introduction to the President.

Question 14th. Who were present at that interview?

Answer. No one, I think, but Messrs. Winslow, Griswold and myself.

Question 15th. Were you present when Mr. Lincoln was before the Naval Board?

Answer. Yes.

Question 16th. What date were you dismissed by Captain Davis' remark to "take the thing home and worship it?"

Answer. The next day after the meeting referred to in question 15th, or possibly the next day but one.

Question 17th. What day did you next call upon Captain Ericsson?

Answer. At the suggestion of Secretary Welles I started for New York that very night, alone, to induce Captain Ericsson to come on to Washington, for everything now depended upon *him*. His presence before the Board was as essential to the adoption of the Monitor as his genius was necessary to her invention. Yet he had been so badly treated by the Government that he declared he never would set foot in Washington again. He was induced, however, to reconsider that decision and went to Washington that night.

Question 18th. Were Winslow and Griswold present at this interview in New York, or did they meet you at any time before Captain Ericsson went to Washington?

Answer. No they were not present, nor did I see them until Ericsson returned from Washington with the verbal order to "go ahead and build her."

Question 19th. When was it agreed that Bushnell, Winslow and Griswold should be sureties and divide profits in four equal shares?

Answer. Bushnell, Winslow and Griswold were not " *sureties* " at all. The agreement between the contractors was made in Washington on the day before the application for letter of introduction to Lincoln was made to Secretary Seward. (See answer to question 11th.) The Government required us to obtain sureties, and these I found in the persons of Hon. N. D. Sperry, of New Haven, and Daniel Drew, of New York.

Question 20th. Were Winslow and Griswold present when Captain Ericsson argued his cause before the Naval Board?

Answer. I cannot say, as I did not myself return with Captain Ericsson.

CAPT. JOHN L. WORDEN,
U. S. NAVY.

LIEUT. S. DANA GREENE,
U. S. NAVY.

So much for your questions. I might add that one week following the return of Ericsson from Washington with the verbal order to "go ahead," I went to Washington and procured a written contract. This contained an unlooked-for conditional clause, requiring us to guarantee the success of the Monitor. To this Mr. Winslow seriously objected. Captain Ericsson and I gave him one week in which to reconsider the matter, another party standing ready to take his place in case he refused to sign the contract. The following week he came down from Troy with Mr. Griswold, and together with Captain Ericsson and myself signed the contract.

Very truly yours,

C. S. BUSHNELL.

MADISON, Conn., August 19, 1885.

I certify that the above is a correct copy.

WILLIAM S. WELLS.

NEW HAVEN, CONN., March 1, 1899.

The following is Mr. Watson's reply:

NEW YORK, August 20, 1885.
150 Nassau street.

HON. C. S. BUSHNELL, ESQ., Madison, Conn.:

Dear Sir:—I have your favor of the 19th in answer to ours of the 15th concerning the Monitor. I thank you for the explicit manner in which you have answered the questions.

Respectfully yours,

EGBERT P. WATSON,
Mechanical Engineer.

A fac-simile of above letter of Egbert P. Watson appears in the Appendix.

The following is an extract from a paper read by Mr. Bushnell before the Army and Navy Club of Connecticut at their annual meeting on June 22, 1894, at the Fort Griswold House, Connecticut. Mr. Bushnell was elected an honorary member of the Club at this meeting. Judge A. B. Beers, of Bridgeport, Conn., was the presiding officer.

Judge Beers: The gentleman to whom the last speaker has so eloquently referred, the Hon. C. S. Bushnell, of New Haven, Conn., is with us to-night as the guest of the Club, and he will tell you how the *Monitor* was built. I introduce the honorable gentleman to you. [Applause.]

MR. BUSHNELL.

Comrades of the Army and Navy Club:

I greet you and am happy to meet you to-night and tell the old old story once again. Lest I weary you by long speech, I have prepared and written out, as particularly and concisely as possible, the simple history. And I think it is fitting, at this place and under the circumstances surrounding us, that I should precede it with a little history of the railroad which preceded the contract for the *Monitor*, and was really the providential cause leading up to it. In the old blue-covered spelling-book, published for so many years by Babcock, and used in all the Connecticut common schools sixty years ago, there were several sage utterances, among which was this: "Old men tell what they have done, young men what they will do, and fools what they can do." The simple and accurate history of the design and construction of the *Monitor*, and the prior events that led up to the historical event at Hampton Roads, by your request are the subjects of my remarks.

* * * * * * * *

"The Rebs were hard at work on the *Merrimac*, a splendid ship, with engine and boilers all complete, and the vessel only waiting for the iron plating. Conferring with Secretary Welles about it, I learned that he had called the attention of Congress to the need of ironclad defence early in the session. He remarked that he would draw up a bill and bring it down to Willard's Hotel that night if I would undertake to engineer it through Congress, which I did quickly, with the help of ex-Governor James E. English, a member of the Naval Committee. A contract for the ironclad *Galena* was at once given me, and William Cramp & Sons, of Philadelphia, received a contract to build the *Ironsides*, a formidable and most useful ship, that did grand service; and how could she help it, when one of the chief officers on board of her was our friend Engineer Wells, now at this board? But it is well known that neither the *Galena* nor the *Ironsides* could be built in time to meet the expected *Merrimac*.

It was claimed by several builders that the *Galena* would not be able to carry the proposed load of iron. I mentioned this to Cornelius H. Delamater, who was in Washington, at Willard's, the day I was awarded the contract for the *Galena*, and he told me to make sure by consulting Capt. John Ericsson, upon whom I called the next day in New York, furnishing him plans and specifications. "Come in to-morrow morning," he said, "and you shall have my decision." The result was as I expected. He declared that the *Galena* would carry the load just as Mr. Pook had figured, and resist a six-inch shot, but he further inquired if I would not like to see and have a plan of an impregnable Battery that could be built in ninety days, most likely in time to meet and destroy the *Merrimac*. My answer was I had been at work for several months to plan and provide an apology for such a boat.

When he opened an old dusty box and unfolded the merits and plans of the little boat in model form, it was less than ten minutes before I fully awoke to the fact that salvation was in store for our Government and country. And I so assured Captain Ericsson. He turned the plans, box and

JOHN F. WINSLOW.

JOHN A. GRISWOLD.

all over to me to handle, just as I desired, saying that I might allow him such interest or compensation as I thought best. I was well aware of the great anxiety of the President, Mr. Lincoln; and Messrs. Seward and Welles were also anxious lest England should join France in recognizing the Confederacy and allowing them belligerent rights, having listened to a discussion on the subject at a reception at the house of Secretary Welles the evening prior. As Secretary Welles went to Hartford the day I came to New York, and as time was the all important factor in that race, I followed him past my home in New Haven, direct to his home in Hartford, and assured him that he need not further worry about foreign interference; I had discovered the means of perfect protection.

He seemed much pleased with my faith in the model, as I was able to explain it to him, and he requested me to lose no time in going to Washington, and have the Board of Navy Officers examine and recommend the plan, and he would come down early in the next week, and give me a contract.

Mind you, this was Friday, and I had not had the plans in hand twenty-four hours, but I started Saturday evening, arriving in Washington Sunday morning, and immediately after breakfast summoned my sub-contractors for the iron work on the Galena to take a quiet ride with me into the suburbs of Washington, and as I went I disclosed to them, Messrs. Winslow and John A. Griswold, of Troy, what a godsend I had found.

I further told them, notwithstanding the intrinsic and priceless value of the plan, we should meet great opposition from old navy prejudice, owing to the sad results of the explosion of the Princeton gun, and the failure of the big caloric ship—Ericsson had cautioned me to beware, on this account, when he turned over the plans. After mature reflection and discussion we decided to call, all together, the next morning (Monday) first on Secretary Seward.

He gave us a very nice letter to President Lincoln, who was more than pleased with the plan, remarking that he knew but little about boats unless it was a flat boat, one of which he was master of in early life. And as the little boat or model we showed him the plan of was flat as need be, he understood the good points from the start, and while he said he had no power in the matter, he would meet us at the office of Admiral Smith at eleven the next morning (Tuesday).

He and we were on hand, big with hope, at the appointed hour and place, and compelled to listen to nothing but disparaging criticism from all the old and young officers of the Navy, with the exception of Admirals Paulding and Smith, two of the Board. Mr. Lincoln sat and listened for nearly an hour to all those opposed could say. Then Admiral Smith turned to the President and asked him what he thought of the novel little plan. Mr. Lincoln arose from his low chair, where he had been so attentively listening and said, "he thought a good deal as the western girl did when she stuck her foot in the stocking, that there was something in it." That was all, and he bade us good morning and left.

On that, Smith and Paulding were ready to recommend the adoption of the plan if Captain Davis, the other member of the Board, would unite with them, but would not take the risk without a unanimous Board. It was in vain that I pleaded the pressing needs of the country. Davis finally told me to take home the plans and worship them, "as they were not like anything in the heavens above, or the earth beneath, or in the waters under the earth." With a sad heart I reported to Secretary Welles. All was dark about me for an hour that Tuesday, but Secretary Welles cheered me up by saying that some influence should be brought to bear on Davis. I caught the idea, and said to him if I could only get Ericsson to come to Washington himself to meet the Board together, in Secretary Welles' room, the magnetism of Ericsson would carry all before him.

I might say to you that I have never met a man possessed of more power to magnetize and carry his audience with him than Captain Ericsson. He got capitalists to put their money into that caloric ship just as freely as water, although it was only an experiment. No one could hope it would be a success, but he wanted to try it. It was a perfect success on a small scale; but when he came to enlarge it, and make a large engine, the expansion and contraction of the metal was such that it was a failure. He and Delamater made $300,000 on those little three-horse power pumping engines, which worked to a charm. I told Secretary Welles that Ericsson had bound himself under oath never to come to Washington until he had been paid by the United States Government his long overdue engineering bill for the Princeton.

Nevertheless I determined to try. I started for New York that Tuesday night, and all the way to Baltimore I thought, "How in the world can I get that man to go, with the state of facts I have to relate?" Then I remembered the flash of his eye and the brightening up of his countenance when he showed me a beautiful gold medal that Louis Napoleon sent him when with England fighting Russia,—the Swedes all hate Russia. In an instant, riding through Baltimore, it came to my mind, "I will get him on his vanity;" and it occurred to me just how I could do it. I went to the Astor House that night, and arrived at his house on Franklin street at exactly nine o'clock the next morning. He did not wait for his girl Ann to come and let me in, but he came himself to the door. Said he, "What is the result?" I said, "Magnificent." "Well," he said, "What?" I said, "Paulding says that your boat would be the thing to punish those Rebels at Charleston." His countenance lit up. I knew then that I had him. I said, "You have a friend in Washington, Commodore Smith; he worships you. He says those plans are worthy of the genius of an Ericsson." Didn't fire come in his eyes? "You see how it works," I said. "Captain Davis wants a little explanation in detail which I could not give." He said, "I will go to-day;" and he started. I did not go with him, mind you. Who do you suppose was the first man he met at the Navy Department? The first man he met was Captain Davis, to whom he said: "I have come down, at the suggestion of Captain Bushnell, to explain about the plan of the *Monitor*," "What," said Davis, "the little plan Bushnell had here Tuesday; why we rejected it *in toto*."

"Rejected it! What for?" said Ericsson. "For want of stability," said Davis. "Stability," roared Ericsson. "No craft that ever floated was more stable than she would be; that is one of her great merits." "Prove it," said Davis, "and we will recommend it at once." "I will go

27

DANIEL DREW.

to my hotel and prepare the proof," said Ericsson, "and meet your Board at the Secretary's room at 1 o'clock." At the hour named he was on hand and showed, as he could easily by diagram, her great stability, and then went on to more fully explain her general merits, closing with the statement that there was offered the perfect means of defence against the *Merrimac*, which could be built in time for the emergency, and no man, unless he was a traitor to his country, would decline to use the means for her safety and defence

Secretary Welles asked the price. Ericsson replied, "$275,000," same as we had named previously. He turned to Admiral Paulding and said, "What do you say?" Paulding said, "I vote to recommend the contract." "And you, Admiral Smith, what do you say?" "I vote for it" said Smith. "And what do you say, Captain Davis?" "I vote for it," said Davis. Then Secretary Welles said to Captain Ericsson, "Go home and start her immediately and send Bushnell down next week for the formal contract."

I had remained in New York, not just fancying the presence of Captain Ericsson when he should first meet Captain Davis, but the result was, as I had expected, most satisfactory.

Messrs. Winslow, Griswold, and myself met Captain Ericsson on his return and ordered everything that could be had to expedite the work and lose no time. This was just eight days after the plans were first shown me and placed in my hands.

Fortunately, we gave the work of building the engine and boilers and all the machinery to C. H. Delmater & Co., who did their utmost to drive the work, and we gave the building of the hull and turret to Thomas F. Rowland.

Mr. Rowland was formerly from Connecticut, and has long been one of the ablest engineers and steamship and gas constructors, and is only known to be loved and respected by friend and acquaintance.

I wish that his health was as strong and vigorous as the speaker, who is a much older man.

Well, I went down to Washington to get the formal contract the next week, as suggested, and lo, a change had come over the spirit of the Board. "Another Ericsson failure," they all predicted, and the only contract I could get recommended was one that required a guarantee of the perfect success of the boat in every particular, or the return of the advance money paid on account. As the work of construction went on, this seemed to me hard terms, but the life of a nation was at stake and Ericsson said go on. Winslow kicked hard, and no one can blame him. Griswold, a splendid man, said if I would get bondsmen to back us, which the government required, they would go on and execute the contract with Captain Ericsson and myself.

Of course I consented, and was able to get Daniel Drew and the Hon. N. D. Sperry, of New Haven, to sign our bond, the latter willing to do almost anything I said was necessary to help the cause. Long may he live, and enjoy the respect of our people.

The result of all this driving work was the getting of this little boat down to Fortress Monroe in the nick of time

Few know that by reason of the great caution of Admiral Dahlgren only fifteen pounds of powder were used at a charge in the 11-inch guns on the *Monitor*.

Captain Ericsson was confident that if thirty pounds had been allowed, instead of fifteen, in her guns, the *Merrimac* would have been sunk inside of thirty minutes after the battle opened. But she did remarkably well as it was, and her memory will be cherished in connection with the officers and men that fought on her, for generations after we are all passed away.

Judge Beers: I move a vote of thanks to Mr. Bushnell for his very able and interesting address.

Carried unanimously, by acclamation.

A Member: I don't like to interrupt the proceedings, but I want to ask Mr. Bushnell one question. It has often been reported that Captain Ericsson never received a cent of bounty or pecuniary compensation. Is there any truth in it? I have read it in the papers over and over again, that Ericsson never received any compensation from the Government.

Mr. Bushnell: It is a matter of history, and everybody should know it, that he was one-fourth interested. I gave him one-fourth, took one-fourth myself, and gave one-fourth to Mr. Griswold, and one fourth to Mr. Winslow. I made him independent through that effort. I have no hesitation in taking a little credit for that. It is, however, a well-known fact that our Government has never yet paid Ericsson for his services as engineer in the construction of the pioneer steam war propeller *Princeton*.

The following is a copy of the original contract with the Government for building the Monitor :

COPY OF CONTRACT WITH THE U. S. GOVERNMENT FOR BUILDING THE " MONITOR."

This Contract, in two parts, made and entered into this Fourth day of October, Anno Domini, One Thousand Eight Hundred and Sixty-one, between *J. Ericsson* of the City of New York, as principal, and John F. Winslow, John A. Griswold and C. S. Bushnell, as sureties on the first part, and *Gideon Welles*, Secretary of the Navy, for and in behalf of the United States on the second part, Witnesseth:—

That in consideration of the payments hereinafter provided for, the party of the first part hereby contracts and agrees to construct an Iron-Clad-Shot-Proof Steam Battery of iron and wood combined on *Ericsson's* plan; the lower vessel to be wholly of iron, and the upper vessel of wood; the length to be one hundred and seventy-nine (179) feet, extreme breadth 41

N. D. SPERRY.

feet and depth 5 feet, or larger, if the party of the first part shall think it
necessary to carry the armament and stores required. The vessel to be
constructed of the best materials and workmanship throughout, according
to the plan and specifications hereto annexed forming a part of this contract; and in addition to said specifications the party of the first part hereby agrees to furnish *masts, spars, sails and rigging* of sufficient dimen-
sions to drive the vessel at the rate of *Six Knots* per hour in a fair breeze
of wind, and the said party of the first part will also furnish in addition to
the said specifications a *Condenser* for making fresh water for the boilers
on the most approved plan. And the party of the first part further contracts and engages that the said vessel shall have proper accommodations
for her stores of all kinds, including provisions for one hundred persons for
ninety days, and shall carry 2500 gallons of water in tanks; that the vessel
shall have a speed of Eight sea miles or knots per hour under steam for
twelve consecutive hours, and carry fuel for her engines for eight day's
consumption at that speed, the deck of the vessel when loaded to be
Eighteen inches above load line amidships; that she shall possess sufficient stability with her armament, stores, and crew on board for safe
sea-service in traversing the Coast of the United States; that her crew shall
be properly accommodated, and that the apparatus for working the Battery
shall prove successful and safe for the purpose intended, and that the vessel, machinery and appointments in all their parts shall work to the entire
satisfaction of the party of the second part.

And the party of the second part hereby agrees to pay for the vessel
completed as aforesaid after trial and satisfactory test the sum of *Two
hundred and seventy-five thousand dollars* in coin or Treasury notes at
the option of the party of the second part in the following manner, to wit —
When the work shall have progressed to the amount of *Fifty thousand*
dollars in the estimation of the Superintendent of the vessel on the part of
the United States, that sum shall be paid to the party of the first part on
certificate of said Superintendent, and thereafter similar payments according to the certificates of said Superintendent, deducting, reserving and
retaining from each and every payment, *Twenty-five per centum*, which
reservation shall be retained until after the completion and satisfactory
trial of the vessel, not to exceed ninety days after she shall be ready
for sea.

And it is further agreed between the said parties that the said
vessel shall be completed in all her parts and appointments for service, and
any omission in these specifications shall be supplied to make her thus
complete ; and in case the said vessel shall fail in performance for speed
for sea-service as before stated, or in the security or successful working of
the turret and guns with safety to the vessel and the men in the turret, or
in her buoyancy to float and carry her Battery as aforesaid, then, and
in that case, the party of the first part hereby bind themselves, their heirs,
executors, administrators and assigns, by these presents, to refund to the
United States the amount of money advanced to them on said vessel
within thirty days after such failure shall have been declared by the party
of the second part, and the party of the first part acknowledge themselves
indebted to the United States in liquidated damages to the full amount of
money advanced as aforesaid.

32

And it is further agreed that the vessel shall be held by the United States as collateral security until said amount of money advanced as aforesaid shall be refunded.

And the party of the first part does further engage and contract that no member of Congress, officer of the navy, or any person holding any office or appointment under the Navy Department, shall be admitted to any share or part of this contract or agreement, or to any benefit to arise thereupon. And it is hereby expressly provided, and this contract is upon this express condition that if any such member of Congress, officer of the navy, or persons above named shall be admitted to any share or part of this contract, or to any benefit to arise under it, or in case the party of the first part shall in any respect fail to perform this contract on their part, the same may be at the option of the United States, declared null and void, without affecting their rights to recover for defaults which may have occurred.

It is further agreed between the said parties that said vessel and equipments in all respects shall be completed and ready for sea in *one hundred days* from the date of this indenture.

Signed, sealed and delivered
in presence of W. L. Barnes
to the signatures of

J. Ericsson.	J. ERICSSON,
John F. Winslow,	JOHN F. WINSLOW,
John A. Griswold.	JOHN A. GRISWOLD,
C. S. Bushnell.	C. S. BUSHNELL.

GIDEON WELLES,
Secretary of the Navy.

Jos. Smith as to signature of G. Welles.

Southern District of New York, SS.

I do hereby certify that in my judgment, John F. Winslow, John A. Griswold and Cornelius S. Bushnell, the sureties in the foregoing contract are sufficient to pay any sum that may be demanded of them in pursuance of the terms thereof. And I further certify, that I have made diligent inquiry before giving this certificate.

C. DELAFIELD SMITH,
U. S. Dist. Atty

NEW YORK, October 4, 1861.

It is understood between the contracting parties that after the Battery shall be ready for sea and be taken possession of by the government for the purpose of testing her properties as stipulated in the contract, such possession shall be regarded as accepting the vessel so far only as the workmanship and quality of materials are concerned, and that the test of the qualities and properities of the vessel as provided shall be made as soon thereafter as practicable, not to exceed ninety days; the reservation of twenty-five per cent. to be withheld until the test is made.

GIDEON WELLES.

Then follows specifications in detail.

SINKING OF THE U. S. FRIGATE "CUMBERLAND" BY THE "MERRIMAC," MARCH 8, 1862.

The following letter verifies the above as being a copy of the original contract:

DEPARTMENT OF THE NAVY BUREAU OF YARDS AND DOCKS,
WASHINGTON, D. C., November 7, 1894.

Dear Sir: Your letter of the 19th ultimo was laid before the Chief of the Bureau, who gave me permission, in the absence of the chief clerk, to make a copy of the contract and specifications of an impregnable and floating battery (the celebrated iron clad) for your personal use, as requested.

I enclose the copy referred to above, and would be pleased to hear if I can further serve you.

Very respectfully,

(Signed)   ROB'T H. YEATMAN,

Clerk.

Mr. W. G. BUSHNELL, New Haven, Conn.

As soon as practicable after this contract of October 4, 1861, was made with the government, the formal contract for building the hull and turret of the vessel, as stated above, by Mr. Bushnell, was made on the 25th of October, 1861, with Thos. F. Rowland, of the Continental Iron Works, at Greenport, L. I.

Mr. Rowland is still active in business, and the writer had the pleasure of an interview with him in his office at the Continental Iron Works on June 14, 1899, at which time he showed me the original contract ; kindly gave me a fac-simile copy of the same, which is, by his permission, printed herewith. The contract reads as follows :

THIS AGREEMENT, made and entered into this twenty-fifth day of October, A. D. 1861, by and between Thomas F. Rowland, Agent, in behalf of the " Continental Iron Works," Greenpoint, Brooklyn, of the first part, and Captain J. Ericsson, of New York; Messrs. John F. Winslow and John A. Griswold, of Troy, N. Y., and C. S. Bushnell, of New Haven Connecticut, parties of the second part.

Witnesseth : That the party of the first part, for and in consideration of a certain sum hereinafter mentioned to be paid to him by the parties of the second part, hereby covenants and agrees to furnish all the tools and facilities, and do all the labor necessary to execute the iron work of an Iron Battery hull (it being understood that the new ship house now being erected is at the expense of the parties of the second part), said Battery to be constructed from the plans and directions which have been or may be furnished the said party of the first part by Captain Ericsson. The party of the first part hereby further agrees to do the said work in a thorough and workmanlike manner and to the entire satisfaction of Captain Ericsson in the shortest possible space of time. And the party of the first part agrees to launch said Battery safely and at his own risk and cost on the East River, then and there * * * * delivering her to the parties of the second part. It is also understood that in consideration of the liberal price hereafter stipulated to be paid by the party of the second part, that in case the work is not prosecuted with all the vigor and energy practicable, then and in that case Captain Ericsson is hereby empowered to instruct the party of the first part to employ a greater number of men or to work a greater number of hours, and which instruction the party of the first part hereby agrees to comply with in order that the work may be completed in the shortest possible space of time as contemplated by this agreement. The parties of the second part hereby agree to furnish all the material for the construction of said Battery, delivering the same at the "Continental Iron Works" as soon as practicable after receiving a specification of the materials required for the construction of said Battery. In consideration of the full and faithful performance of these presents by the party of the first part, the parties of the second part hereby covenant and agree to pay the party of the first part the sum of seven and one-half (7½) cents per pound (net weight) of iron used in the construction of said hull by the party of the first part, payments to be made weekly in proportion to the progress of the work, the balance remaining to be paid when the hull is launched. The parties to this instrument hereby mutually agree that should any alteration in the plans furnished by Captain Ericsson be desired after the same have been executed, the party of the first part shall make any alterations that may be deemed desirable by Captain Ericsson at the expense of the parties of the second part.

Witness the hands and seals of the said parties the day and year before written.

J. ERICSSON,   [SEAL]

J. F. WINSLOW,   [SEAL]

JOHN A. GRISWOLD,   [SEAL]

                                      [SEAL]

THOS. F. ROWLAND, *Agent*   [SEAL]

Witness to the signature of J. Ericsson :
    C. W. MacCord.

Witness to the signatures of J. F. Winslow and John A. Griswold :
    F. Ellis.

Witness to the signature of T. F. Rowland :
    Warren E. Hill.

It will be observed that the place in above sub-contract is vacant where Mr. Bushnell's signature should appear. He was a very busy man at this period and doubtless could not be present when this sub-contract was executed with the builder, for it is observed that his name appears in the text of the contract as one of the parties of the second part.

THE U. S. S. "GALENA."

SAMUEL H. POOK,
Naval Constructor.

In the foregoing several statements of Mr. Bushnell it is observed that he refers to a bond exacted by the Government as surety for money advanced in the building of the Monitor. Search has been made for this bond, but thus far without finding it. The following correspondence with Hon. N. D. Sperry, our present member of Congress, and the surviving bondsman, will set the question of this bond at rest:

New Haven, Conn., June 3, 1899.

Hon. N. D. Sperry, City.

My Dear Sir :—You will recall I stated to you a few days ago, that although search has been made for the bond that you and Daniel Drew signed, still it has not yet been found, and may not be.

Therefore, in lieu of this document, in case it does not come to light, I wish you would kindly write me how it was that you went on the bond with Daniel Drew, and the nature of the bond.

I wish the letter for publication (with your permission) in my pamphlet, in connection with the other data and documents I have relating to Mr. Bushnell and the building of the " Monitor."

Yours very truly,
WM. S. WELLS.

New Haven, Conn., June 9, 1899.

Mr. William S. Wells, New Haven, Conn.:

My Dear Sir :—Your letter of the 3d inst. duly received. I dislike to give out anything for publication in relation to the bond referred to, as Mr. Bushnell's reference to it should be sufficient.

I will, however, at your request, state that I was asked by Mr. Bushnell to go upon the bond in question, simply as surety to the government for money advanced in building the " Monitor," and the conditions specified in the Government contract.

I remember it was on Sunday, March 9, the day of the battle of the " Monitor " and the " Merrimac," that I was in the office of the *Journal and Courier* here in New Haven with Mr. Bushnell and others, receiving news as the encounter was taking place. When word came that the " Monitor " had whipped the " Merrimac," Mr. Bushnell, who was at my side slapped his hands on my shoulders vigorously and said. " My dear friend Sperry, your bond is safe."

There was great rejoicing at that moment, and many remarked that if it had not been for the construction of this little vessel just in the nick of time, the " Merrimac " could have laid the whole coast under contribution.

Mr. Bushnell's address before the Army and Navy Club of Connecticut, together with other documents I have seen, should, in the absence of the bond at this time, forever set at rest any questions that might arise in regard to such a bond having been made and signed by Daniel Drew and myself.

Very truly yours,
N. D. SPERRY.

35

In the foregoing story by Mr. Bushnell, it will be observed that he does not claim to have built the vessel, did not perform the mechanical work, but accords full credit and appreciation of those who gave support to his undertaking.

He had not only to contend with opposition at the inception of the project, but the question of mechanical skill and materials was one of the most vital importance to success. This difficulty, like others, was effectually overcome, for it will be observed that he states in his letter to Hon. Gideon Welles, "I secured at once the co-operation of Hon. John A. Griswold and John F. Winslow, of Troy, large manufacturers of iron plates." It will be seen also in the contract with Thomas F. Rowland of the Continental Iron Works, that the "parties of the second part" were to "furnish all the materials for the construction of said battery, delivering the same at the Continental Iron Works." Therefore to Mr. Griswold and Mr. Winslow much credit is due for the substantial aid that admitted of the vessel's construction.

When the prow of the Merrimac was finally turned toward Norfolk after her defeat, and the news was flashed over the land, the beginning of the end of the war could be reasonably inferred, for new hope came to the loyal hearts of the country; a ray of light came from the gloom, stimulating the nation to renewed activity. Men rushed to the ranks to defend the rightful supremacy of our flag, and the wealth of our people was poured into our treasury for a vigorous prosecution of the war to a glorious termination.

After this battle of the Monitor and Merrimac, the navies of the world had to be at once rebuilt on new lines, the old defences became obsolete, and the vast development of armaments and the stimulus given to the production and working of iron and steel may be truly dated from the building of the Monitor.

To John Ericsson's talent we owe a debt of gratitude, but his invention was of no practical value until another more bold and resourceful appeared who developed the ideas of the inventor's mind. In referring to this battle we must not be unmindful of Capt. John L. Worden and his gallant crew, and appreciative remembrance should be had of Lieut. S. Dana Greene, who fought the ship to a final success after Captain Worden had been wounded.

In monarchial countries, one who performed such a service as Mr. Bushnell did would have received royal favors. Decorations and honorable titles would have been bestowed in profusion, and sculptors would have been busy in erecting monuments to his memory.

Let us, sovereigns of a great nation, be not unmindful of our duty to a great benefactor of our country and the world. We neglected him and failed to appreciate him living. Let us now make amends for our blindness or indifference and bend our energies to erect to him a suitable memorial in New Haven, the city of his home, that will be in some measure commemorative of our gratitude for his devoted, generous, self-sacrificing and patriotic life, and a fit testimonial of our appreciation of what he has done for the good of our whole people, and the benefit of the entire world, by his rare and beneficent public service.

NEW HAVEN, CONN.,
September, 1899.

Wm. S. Wells.

39

"MONITOR."   "GALENA."

WITH U. S. GUNBOATS ON JAMES RIVER COVERING RETREAT.

Col. David Torrance, President of the Army and Navy Club and Associate Judge of the Supreme Court of Connecticut, paid a beautiful tribute to the memory of Mr. Bushnell, as follows :

Extract from report of annual meeting, held at New London, June 26, 1896.

Referring to the Death Roll, the Honorable David Torrance, President of the Club, spoke as follows :—

"And among the latest to go, only last month, was one, an honorary member, by no means the least in our regard and esteem, one to whom only two years ago we listened with such pleasure as he told the simple story of his connection with the Monitor. You have not forgotten that dismal Saturday in March, 1862, when the Merrimac, steaming from behind Crane's Island, annihilated our navy in an hour; crushing the Cumberland like an egg shell, and sending her gallant crew to the bottom; burning the Congress to the water's edge, and steaming back to her anchorage with colors flying, unhurt of all our batteries. Naval architecture and naval ordnance had been revolutionized since noon. Our ships were as paper, our cannon as pop-guns. The monster could laugh at our forts and frigates. And there it was, ready on the morrow, flushed with victory, conscious of power, to go wherever the waters would float her, resistless as fate, to raise the blockade, to bombard New York, to sweep our commerce from the seas. As we took in the full meaning of that afternoon's work, did not the bravest shudder for what the morning might bring? But at eventide there was light. About ten o'clock that night the little "cheesebox on a raft" was towed into Hampton Roads. The Government had not built her nor paid for her, and the red tape of the naval bureaus had all but laughed her to scorn. But there she was, in the very nick of time; and on Sunday, after a terrible conflict, she sent the Merrimac back to her anchorage, wounded to death, never more to work us harm.

How came the Monitor there at that opportune moment? You heard the story two years ago. It was chiefly because a Connecticut Yankee, months before, had the sagacity to perceive, in the small model shown to him by the Swedish genius, the vessel for the hour; and not only the sagacity to perceive, but the influence, the pluck, the grit, the persistence, to force the Government to give it a trial, and patriotic enough and having faith enough in his judgment to back it with all his capital. All honor to the Monitor and her gallant commander and crew. All honor to the genius that modeled her and built her. But let us not forget to add, all honor to the man who was so largely instrumental in placing her where she would do the most good at the right time, Cornelius S. Bushnell."

APPENDIX.

43

New York March 2ᵈ 1877

My Dear Sir.

I have read with much
pleasure your father's statement to Mr Willes
concerning the construction of the Original
monitor. I do not think that any changes
or additions are needed, the main facts
being well stated

Allow me to call your attention to
the fact that your name should be spelt
with a single r.

Please find your father's paper enclosed.
Yours very truly
J. Ericsson

Ericsson F Bushnell Esq
New Haven

44

Hartford

C. S. Bushnell Esq — 19th March 1877

My Dear Sir

I received on the
16th inst your interesting communication, without date — relative
to the construction of the Monitor.
Many of the incidents narrated
by you I remember, although
more than fifteen years have
gone by since they transpired.
Some errors, not very essential
are caused by lapse of years, occur.
— Sedgwick, not Kin, was Chairman
of the Naval Committee — Griswold
resided in Troy, not New York,
and subsequently represented the
Troy District in Congress. &c.

I will remember asking you

to put in writing the facts
in your possession concerning
the Construction of the Monitor.
Some statements of Gen Butler,
Wendell Phillips, and others
to disparage the Department,
pervert the truth and deny
us all credit. led Admiral
Smith, in the Autumn of 1862
to address to me a communication,
reciting the facts, for, he said,
when we were gone, those
of us who took the responsibility
and would have incurred the
disgrace had Ericsson's invention
proved a failure, would be
ignored and history mistated,
'As you were more intimate
with the case at its inception — were

the first to bring it to the attention of the Department, it seems to me proper that your recollection & knowledge of the transaction should be reduced to writing. I am greatly obliged to you for the full an satisfactory manner in which you have complied with my request. Next, after Ericsson himself, you are entitled to the credit of bringing his invention to the knowledge of the Department. I would not, knowingly, do injustice to any one, and I am well aware that the officers in civil life, and who in administering the government directs movements by which naval and military men acquire renown is often by the

47

passing multitude while thought
of our scarcely known, but
the truth should not be suppressed.

The civilians of the Navy
Department who accepted and
pursued through ridicule and
assault the Monitor experiment,
Butler and others would slight or
defame — In the history of
the War, the Navy Department,
which originated, planned and
carried forward the naval
achievements from Hatteras to
their Island, and finally Fort
Fisher is scarcely known or
mentioned. The heroes who
fought the battles and perilled their
lives to carry into effect the plans
which the Dept' devised are deservedly
honorable remembrance — but the originators
are many are little known.

I remember, my dear Sir, your earnest
efforts in the early days of the War, and the
comfort they gave me. Very Gideon Welles

THE MECHANICAL ENGINEER.

Marine — Stationary Engineering,

The Trade Medium for the Shop and Engine Room.

130 Nassau st New York Aug 20 1885.

Hon C S Bushnell Esq,

    Madison Tenn

Dear Sir

    I have your favor of the
19th in answer to ours of the
15th concerning the elevator
I thank you for the explicit
manner in which you have
answered the questions

    Respy yrs

    Frank F Watson.

Editor Mech. Engr

United States of America

Washington City Guards Armory.

Head Qrs, Washington, D. C., April 27, 1861.

To Hon. S. Cameron, Secretary of War, U. S.

Sir: The undersigned, General Maj, a Guards Battalion, ... the Capitol of the United States ...

...

(signatures)
James W. Nye, Major Commanding
David Webb, Capt. 1st Company
J. C. Winters, Capt. 2d Company.

War Department, May 2, 1861.

Major James W. Nye:

Sir: In reply to your letter of the 27th of April, stating that, in consequence of the arrival of large numbers of troops in this city, the exigencies have ceased ... the Battalion ... and that you would be pleased, therefore, to have authority to disband the battalion and have an honorable discharge from ...

Concurring fully with you, I enable grant to the ... extend you, and through you to the men under your command, the assurance of my high appreciation of the very prompt and patriotic manner in which your battalion was organized for the defense of the Capital, and its ... services rendered by it during the hour of its existence.

Very respectfully,

Simon Cameron

I cheerfully concur in the foregoing to hereunto given by the Hon. Secretary of War.

May 2, 1861.

A. Lincoln

By authority vested in me as Major of the **Washington City Battalion**, I, DAVID WEBB, now commanding, do hereby certify that *Cornelius D. Bushnell* a Member of said Battalion, served his Country in defense of the **National Capital**, at a time of great peril, when threatened by hordes of traitors: and service commencing on the eighteenth day of April, 1861, and ending on the date hereof.

I also, by virtue of said authority, do hereby **HONORABLY DISCHARGE** the said *C. D. Bushnell* from the service of the **United States**.

Given under my hand, at **Washington City**, this *fourth* day of May, 1861.

David Webb
Major Commanding

T. S. Littlejohn
Adjutant

THE CORNELIUS S. BUSHNELL NATIONAL MEMORIAL ASSOCIATION.

Organized March 9, 1899.

The 36th Anniversary of the battle between the Monitor and Merrimac.

President:—NORRIS G. OSBORN, Editor New Haven Daily *Register*, New Haven, Conn.

Vice Presidents:—Hon. WILLIAM E. SIMONDS, Past Dept. Commander Conn. Grand Army of the Republic.

FRANCIS E. ALLEN, Past Junior Vice Commander-in-Chief, G. A. R., Hartford, Conn.

Gen. E. S. GREELEY, Vice President Yale National Bank, New Haven, Conn.

WILLIAM S. WELLS, Late Second Assistant Engineer, U. S. N., New Haven, Conn.

Hon. N. D. SPERRY, Member of Congress, New Haven, Conn.

S. J. FOX, Late Assistant Adjutant General of Conn., New Haven, Conn.

Secretary:—GEORGE H. FORD, New Haven, Conn.

Assistant Secretary:—JOHN M. CRAMPTON, New Haven, Conn.

Second Assistant Secretary:—WILLARD C. WARREN, New Haven, Conn.

Treasurer:—New Haven Trust Company, T. ATTWATER BARNES, President, New Haven, Conn.

Historian:—WILLIAM S. WELLS, Late Second Assistant Engineer, U. S. N., and Past National Commander-in-Chief of the Naval Veterans of the United States, New Haven, Conn.

FINANCE AND SUBSCRIPTION COMMITTEE.

E. E. BRADLEY, New Haven, Conn.

S. E. MERWIN, New Haven, Conn.

E. G. STODDARD, New Haven, Conn.

PHELPS MONTGOMERY, New Haven, Conn.

EDWARD C. BEECHER, New Haven, Conn.

FRANK T. LEE, New Haven, Conn.

FRANCIS E. HUNS, New Haven, Conn.

EDWARD S. SWIFT, New Haven, Conn.

BENJAMIN R. ESGLISH, New Haven, Conn.

EDWARD A. BOWERS, New Haven, Conn.

COMMITTEE ON DESIGN.

PROF. JOHN F. WEIR, *Chairman.*
L. W. ROBINSON,
GEORGE D. SEYMOUR,
HON. N. D. SPERRY,
HON. C. T. DRISCOLL,
EVERETT E. LORD,
HENRY T. BLAKE.

PRESS COMMITTEE.

C. W. PICKETT, *Chairman.*
WILLIAM G. PRATT,
JOHN D. JACKSON,
LEWIS S. WELCH,
LEO. R. HAMMOND,
J. B. LUCKE,
WIEGAND SCHLEIN,
ALEXANDER TROUP,
F. W. BARBER,
ALBERT BARCLAY,
JAMES F. SCOTT.

COMMITTEE ON PRINTING.

WILSON H. LEE, *Chairman.*
ISAAC BROMLEY,
JOHN H. PLATT,
JOHN C. NORTH,
GEORGE W. LEWIS.

GENERAL COMMITTEE.

MAX ADLER, *Chairman.*

There are many gentlemen of this City, State and United States on the General Committee.

NOTE.

This pamphlet will show you to whom we are really indebted for the timely and fortunate construction of the now famous and initial iron war vessel, the "Monitor."

The people of this country owe a patriotic debt of gratitude to the spirit and energy that induced the government to build the vessel which defeated the "Merrimac" at Hampton Roads on March 9, 1862.

The Cornelius S. Bushnell National Memorial Association believes the reader will be only too glad of the opportunity to show his substantial appreciation of what Cornelius S. Bushnell did to lift the gloom which hung over our land in one of the darkest days of our country's history.

It is planned to erect a suitable memorial to Mr. Bushnell, at New Haven, Conn., the city of his home, at an estimated cost of $25,000.

The State of Connecticut has contributed $5,000 towards the expense. After reading this pamphlet, we believe you will gladly contribute to the fund.

Contributions may be sent to the Treasurer, the "New Haven Trust Co." (T. Attwater Barnes, President), First National Bank Building, New Haven, Conn.

AVEN, CONN.,
ber, 1899.